AF225728

POSTCARD HISTORY SERIES

Johnson City

STATE FLAG OF TENNESSEE. Col. Le Roy Reeves, a native of Johnson City born June 23, 1876, proposed his design for an official state flag to legislators who sponsored the bill for approval of the flag that passed on April 17, 1905. He described his design as follows: "The three stars are of pure white, representing the three grand divisions of the state. They are bound together by the endless circle of the blue field, the symbol being bound together in one—an indissoluble trinity." The state flag was first flown over East Tennessee State Normal School in Johnson City on October 10, 1911. (Author's collection.)

ON THE FRONT COVER: STREET SCENE. This c. 1940s Cline real-photo postcard (RPPC), with a view looking east on Main Street at the intersection of Buffalo Street just beyond Fountain Square, shows a vibrant, bustling downtown. Visible in the foreground is the Anderson Drug Store in the old Unaka and City National Bank Building where Freiberg's German Restaurant is located today. Also visible are the Jones Vance and Snyder Jones Pharmacies, Fields Clothing and Hardware, Boston Shoe Shop, Parks-Belk, Dossers, Southern Shoes, and Sterchi's. (Author's collection.)

ON THE BACK COVER: SHOWING CANNON AT SOLDIERS HOME. In the early days, this cannon, possibly a Civil War 6-pounder, was kept on display to one side of the flagpole across the street from the mess hall. The two-wheeled wagons behind the cannon are limbers, and the four-wheeled wagons are caissons; both were used for carrying ammunition boxes. The caissons were used at times to carry caskets to the cemetery. (Author's collection.)

POSTCARD HISTORY SERIES

Johnson City

L. Thomas Roberts

ARCADIA PUBLISHING

*Oh, the depth of the riches and wisdom and knowledge of God!
How unsearchable are his judgments and how inscrutable his
ways! For from him and through him and to him are all things.
To him be glory forever. Amen. Romans 11:33 and 36*

*To Joyce, my wife, best friend, and partner in this
journey of life, for the inspiration she gives me each day
with her smile, kindness, warmth, and beauty*

*In memory of my grandparents Win and "Preacher" Roberts,
who brought our family to Johnson City in 1947, and Virginia
and Arthur Clockadale, who allowed my mom to go away to
East Tennessee State College where my parents met*

CONTENTS

ACKNOWLEDGMENTS

This postcard history of Johnson City would not have been possible or as interesting if it weren't for the contributions of many other Johnson Citians that have shared their love of our city's history in print and online. Samuel Cole Williams and Ray Stahl's histories of Johnson City, Johnny Graybeal's *The Railroads of Johnson City*, and the Washington County Historical Association's *History of Washington County* were invaluable. The extensive writing of Bob L. Cox and his online material in Bob Cox's Yesteryear are a delight and inspiration to read, providing insight on much of the area's history. Prior to Mr. Cox's online postings, my dad would save his columns from the Johnson City paper for me to read and discuss with him on my visits back home. I keep those columns saved alongside Tom Hodges's columns that feature Johnson City area history. Other helpful web resources that document the history of Johnson City include *Johnson's Depot*; *Johnson City, Tennessee Memories*; *You Know You Went to ETSU If...*; and *Memories of Mountain Home VA – Employees, Families and Friends*. The shared recollections, stories, and photographs on these sites has made our history accessible in ways our ancestors could never have imagined, and their reminiscences have enriched this book.

I am also grateful for the efforts of Mildred Kozsuch (former historian for Washington County) to preserve Johnson City's postcards through the publication of *Thirty-Six Old Picture Postcards of Elizabethton, Johnson City and Jonesboro* and the preservation of her postcard collection in the Archives of Appalachia. I had the pleasure of meeting Mrs. Kozsuch for the first time at the Washington County, Tennessee, archives dedication on April 1, 2017, not long before she passed in June. Another local historian I would like to remember here is Frank Tannewitz Jr., who taught business classes and served as guidance counselor at Science Hill from 1948 to 1985 and loved our local history. I was honored to pick up several old photographs and postcards from his collection after he passed, and I enjoy being able to share some of them in this publication as well as online. All of the images in this book come from the author's collection unless noted otherwise.

A special thank-you goes to Alan Bridwell, Roger Benfield, Ted Bowers, and Ned Irwin, Washington County archivist, for the time they took to review my manuscript and to find answers to questions I had not resolved. Many thanks are given to Martha Whaley, the History of Medicine Librarian at ETSU, for taking time out of her day to give me a tour of the Museum at Mountain Home and for the information she provided. Thanks also go to the staff members at the Archives of Appalachia for their assistance during my visits to the archive to look through boxes of materials and to Lindsay Kenderes, information resources librarian and college archivist for the P.H. Welshimer Memorial Library at Milligan College, for being so gracious with her time during my visit to the library. Thanks go to George Prater of Prater Collectibles in Clayton, Georgia, for assisting me with the procurement of rare postcards for the book. I also wish to thank my title managers at Arcadia Publishing, Liz Gurley and Caitrin Cunningham, for their patience with me during the production of this book.

Most of all, thank you to my wife and our children, Jennifer, Katie, Ben, Brody and Chaz, for your love and patience while I stumbled over many hurdles during completion of this project.

INTRODUCTION

Imagine thousands of buffalo roaming through the Tennessee backcountry. These massive herds trampled a deep, open trail through the forest over time. The Great Buffalo Trail, or Trace, was used by Indians and followed by the first Englishmen to visit the area, James Needham and Gabriel Arthur. They were sent out from Fort Henry by Col. Abraham Wood in 1673 to explore the Great Valley of East Tennessee and establish a trading path with the Cherokee. This trail followed Buffalo Creek and went around the end of Buffalo Mountain past the land and spring on what would become the Tipton-Haynes farm.

By the late 1700s, frontiersmen such as Daniel Boone, William Bean, Joseph Tipton, Robert Young, John and Landon Carter, and John Sevier crossed the mountains into Cherokee land to inhabit present-day upper East Tennessee. They built homes along local waterways such as Boones Creek and Sinking Creek, and the Watauga, Holston, and Nolichucky Rivers. In 1772, these early settlers created the Watauga Association to oversee the protection and development of the settlements. In 1784, the state of Franklin was formed in present-day Washington County (the first capital was in Jonesborough) after North Carolina ceded the land to the United States Congress in April 1784. John Sevier, a Revolutionary War veteran, was chosen governor of this short-lived independent state located in present-day upper East Tennessee. This new, separate but unofficial state contained four original counties—Washington, Sullivan, Spencer, and Greene—and annexed four counties in 1785—Wayne, Caswell, Sevier, and Blount—before the state was dissolved and rejoined North Carolina in 1789. Shortly thereafter, the area would be incorporated into the Territory South of the River Ohio. The home of William Cobb, Rocky Mount, was used by Gov. William Blount to conduct the business of the new territory. From 1790 to 1792, Rocky Mount served as the first capital. In 1796, the region was incorporated into the new state of Tennessee with John Sevier as the state's first governor.

During this time, the area to become Johnson City was farmland owned by the Tipton and Jobe families and was known as the Brush Creek Settlement. Over the next century, upper East Tennessee slowly continued to develop, with the Johnson City area remaining agricultural. However, the arrival of a new mode of transportation, railroads, would soon transform the isolated farmland along Brush Creek into a center of commerce and agriculture. As a member of the 27th General Assembly (1847–1849), Landon Carter Haynes introduced a bill to incorporate the East Tennessee & Virginia (ET&V) Railroad, which was chartered in 1849. The proposed route went from Knoxville, Tennessee, to Bristol, Virginia. On September 8, 1852, a contract was signed for the grade preparation through the portion of Washington County that would become Johnson City.

The earliest documentation of Henry Johnson in the area is his marriage to Mary Ann Hoss in Washington County on February 23, 1834. In December 1846, he purchased 100 acres on Sinking Creek and operated a mill there and was listed as the postmaster of Blue Plum from 1849 to 1855. On May 31, 1854, he purchased half an acre of land from Abraham Jobe on Brush Creek, located at the intersection of the recently graded ET&V rail line and the stage road connecting Jonesborough to Elizabethton (present-day Market Street). Clearly, he understood the potential for the property at this intersection, but his future investment here presented a great risk as well. Johnson quickly built a combination home, store, and waiting room; and in 1856, prior to track being laid in this area in the spring of 1857, he constructed a brick two-story multipurpose restaurant, inn, and depot. Train service to his depot, Johnson's Depot, began on July 4, 1857. A week later, the Post Office Department established a post office at the depot and named Johnson postmaster.

In 1857, another early entrepreneur, Thomas Faw, established a rival store and house on land purchased from Tipton Jobe located along the stage line, and the little community of Johnson's Depot began to expand, serving as a stopover for passengers and freight on the railroad. In 1859, Johnson supported Thomas A.R. Nelson in his run for Congress against Landon Carter Haynes. Nelson won by a few votes and a bitter Haynes pulled strings with the Post Office Department in Washington and had the name of the post office changed to Haynesville, with Johnson removed as postmaster on October 8, 1859. Thomas Faw would serve as postmaster in 1860, with the post office likely located in his store. During this time, Johnson interceded with Congressman Nelson, and the name of the post office was changed back to Johnson's Depot on April 9, 1861.

During the Civil War, the town was called Haynesville while Confederate forces were in control of the area, despite three-fifths of military-aged men joining the Union army, including two of Henry Johnson's sons. In the postwar period, other businesses followed, and on December 1, 1869, incorporation of the first town charter was received, with the name being changed to Johnson City for Johnson's efforts in developing the area. In 1881, the East Tennessee & Western North Carolina (ET&WNC) Railroad came to Johnson City and the following year the line reached Cranberry, North Carolina, and its deposits of iron ore, which generated new industry for the area. Johnson City officials wanted to attract a third railroad to the city to further establish the area as an iron-manufacturing center, so they purchased bonds from the Charleston, Cincinnati, and Chicago (3Cs) Railroad Company, led by General John T. Wilder. The new railway attracted investors to the area, which led to the development of the Carnegie Land and Improvement Company, the Carnegie Furnace Company, and the Carnegie Hotel.

With three railroads, Johnson City grew from 605 residents in 1880 to 4,645 citizens in 1890. Johnson City had become a "New South boomtown." The boom of the 1880s gave way to a serious depression with the Panic of 1893, which caused the 3Cs Railroad to fold along with the Carnegie Furnace Company and the Carnegie Land Company. With the eventual recovery of the economy came opportunity for new investors to pick up the pieces of the 3Cs. The Southern and Western Railway Company (S&W), led by George L. Carter, expanded the 3Cs and other lines to Spartanburg, South Carolina, and Elkhorn City, Kentucky, in 1905, changing the name in 1908 to the Carolina, Clinchfield and Ohio (CC&O) Railroad. With three successful rail lines operating in the area, Johnson City continued to thrive and the population grew from 8,562 in 1910 to 25,080 in 1930, transforming the town into an even greater regional commercial center. From the late 1800s forward, the downtown footprint took shape, with many of the historic buildings present today constructed in the early 1900s.

Starting with examples from America's obsession with postcards in the early 1900s, the following pages present a snapshot of the postcards from Johnson City's past, with a look back at the people, places, and activities around the Greater Johnson City area.

One

FROM FRONTIER LAND TO RAILROAD CITY

PORTRAIT OF DANIEL BOONE. Daniel Boone (1734–1820) is probably the best-known American frontiersmen whose exploits crossing the Appalachian Mountains to hunt and explore made him one of the first folk heroes of the United States. Boone was born in Oley, Berks County, Pennsylvania. He was the sixth child of Quaker parents. During his exploits in the United States' western territory, he passed through the area that would become Johnson City and, for a short time, relocated his family to the Watauga settlements.

BOONE'S FALLS. On one of his excursions through this area, Boone was chased by Indians and hid underneath these falls, which were then about four feet high, to escape capture. The falls and creek were named for Boone, who was the namesake for the community that later sprang up around this area. (Frank Tannewitz Jr. collection.)

"D. BOONE CILLED A BARR . . . 1760." This beech tree, known as the Daniel Boone Tree, contained an inscription left by Boone during one of his trips through the area. The tree, believed to have been over 350 years old and the last known surviving Boone Bear Tree, fell during a storm in 1920. However, portions of the tree lived on when the John Sevier Chapter of the Daughters of the American Revolution created gavels from a portion of the tree.

MASSENGILL MEMORIAL MONUMENT. Erected by the Sons of the American Revolution, this monument depicts Henry and Mary Massengill and honors them and their family who traveled from North Carolina to the Watauga Settlement in 1769. The statute stood from 1937 to 1990 in north Johnson City at the intersection of the Bristol and Kingsport highways until a road improvement project required relocation of the 24-foot statue to its current site in Winged Deer Park.

TENNESSEE STATE SHRINE. Rocky Mount, the home of William Cobb, the brother of Mary Cobb Massengill, was the first capitol of the Southwest Territory. William Blount, the governor of the Territory South of the River Ohio, presided over the newly formed territory from 1790 to 1792. The home is now part of a living history museum complex located on Highway 11E in Piney Flats.

CABIN MARKING BIRTHPLACE OF DAVY CROCKETT. Davy Crockett, one of the outstanding pioneers of Tennessee, was born August 17, 1786, in a cabin at this location near Limestone, about 14 miles from Johnson City. Prior to his death at the Alamo, he was a trapper, explorer, and scout, a member of the state legislature, and a representative in Congress.

12

TIPTON-HAYNES FARM. Located at 2620 South Roan Street, the Tipton-Haynes house and farm are a state historic site that includes a house originally built in 1784 by Col. John Tipton (1730–1813) and ten other buildings. In 1839, Landon Carter Haynes (1816–1875) received the farm as a wedding present from his father. As a state senator, Haynes helped obtain funding for railroad construction. During the Civil War, he was elected to the Confederate Senate but lost his home during the war and fled to Memphis to escape Unionist reprisals.

JOHNSON'S DEPOT. The beginning of Johnson City can be traced back to the creation of the East Tennessee & Virginia Railroad, which later became the Southern. Henry Johnson took a risk that the ET&V would be successful and built a depot with a water tank as well as a store, post office, and home at the junction of the proposed railroad and the southwest corner of the Stage Road. (Frank Tannewitz Jr. collection.)

MAKING A CUT. This postcard from Johnson City postmarked October 23, 1909, depicts a steam shovel and crew loading material removed from a cut in the hillside to horse-drawn wagons. Many scenes such as this occurred during construction of rail lines and bridges in the area.

SOUTHERN PASSENGER STATION. On July 1, 1894, the East Tennessee, Virginia, & Georgia Railroad merged with the Richmond & Danville Railroad to form the Southern Railway. The Southern expanded through the acquisition of numerous rail lines and companies, making it one of the most extensive railway systems in the nation. Of the three railway companies serving Johnson City, the Southern was the largest and offered more connections.

ET&WNC Depot. The East Tennessee & Western North Carolina Railroad (ET&WNC) was officially organized in February 1868, but funding issues delayed opening to the public until August 22, 1881, with one train per day running between Johnson City and Hampton. The following year, on July 3, the route was opened to Cranberry, North Carolina, completing the project and the ET&WNC goal to ship iron ore and lumber out of the mountains. Today, the depot is home to the White Duck Taco Company and Yee-Haw Brewing. (Frank Tannewitz Jr. collection.)

"Tweetsie." The nickname "Tweetsie" was given by area residents who became accustomed to the shrill "tweet" of the locomotive whistles that echoed through the mountains. The nickname stuck and was used interchangeably with the ET&WNCs official name. Special excursion trains would pause at Pardee Point in the heart of the gorge, and passengers would disembark to take in the sheer cliffs rising hundreds of feet above the rushing river.

"HALFWAY JOHNSON CITY TO CRANBERRY." Pardee Point, named for the Pardee family who helped finance the railway with Ario Pardee Jr. serving as president, was located at mile marker 17 along the ET&WNC railway. This stop was the midpoint from a total number of stops as well as a time standpoint. The train would leave Johnson City at 7:45 a.m. and this was the seventh out of fourteen stops prior to the terminus in Cranberry, where the train was scheduled to arrive at 11:00 a.m.

THROUGH THE GORGE ON THE ET&WNC. The Doe River Gorge was the scenic gem of a trip on the "Tweetsie." After the train left Hampton, it went upgrade and shortly afterwards passed through the tunnel that led into the gorge. The narrow-gauge line closed on October 16, 1950, and the last standard-gauge steam engine ran until 1967.

"IN GORGE ON S. & W. RY." Starting as the Charleston, Cincinnati, and Chicago (3Cs) Railroad in 1886, led by Gen. John T. Wilder, it was completed over 30 years later as the Carolina, Clinchfield & Ohio (CC&O) Railroad, led by George L. Carter. Prior to Carter's involvement, the 3Cs failed during the Panic of 1893, a serious economic depression in the United States. It was taken over by the Ohio River & Charleston Railway (OR&C), formed in 1894. Investors led by Carter bought tracks from Johnson City to Boonford, North Carolina, in June 1902 and named their route the South & Western Railway (S&W).

"SCENE ON THE C.C. & O." The S&W was renamed the Carolina, Clinchfield & Ohio (CC&O) Railroad in 1908 but is best known as the Clinchfield Railroad. It ran from 1902 until 1983, crossing the Appalachian Mountains and opening the communities along its 277-mile route to industry and commerce. The track stretched from the northern terminus at Elkhorn City, Kentucky, which was completed on June 12, 1915, through Virginia, Tennessee, and North Carolina, to the southern terminus in Spartanburg, South Carolina, completed on Friday, October 29, 1909.

"Trestle on the C.C.& O. Ry." With maximum grades of 1.5 percent and maximum curves of 14 degrees, the CC&O was considered the best-engineered and -built line in the South, which gave it a significant competitive advantage hauling coal. This feat of construction came at a steep cost, with the cutting of many tunnels and the building of many bridges to maintain the railway's standards.

CC&O Depot. The depot, located at 300 Buffalo Street and now restored as the Tupelo Honey Café, was built in 1908 with two sections: a two-story passenger station and a one-story freight house/depot. The depot was used as a passenger station until 1955 and as a yard office until the 1970s. Listed in the National Register of Historic Places in 2008, it is the only intact depot of the three railroads in town. (Frank Tannewitz Jr. collection.)

Two

MOUNTAIN HOME, A CITY WITHIN A CITY

"SOLDIERS HOME." Over 1,000 workers were employed for the initial three-year construction period of the compound designed to be a self-sufficient city within a city. The original construction included 37 buildings at the cost of $3 million. There were eight barracks for 2,500 men, a mess hall, a four-ward infirmary, officers'/surgeons' quarters, administrative building, powerhouse, greenhouse, icehouse, laundry, dairy department, hotel, chapel, theater, bandstand, jail, and morgue. The grounds became a tourist attraction, which was facilitated by the trolley line running 10 hours per day at 5¢ each way.

W. P. BROWNLOW, M. C.

WALTER P. BROWNLOW AND HIS FUNERAL. Congressman Walter Preston Brownlow (1851–1910) was instrumental in establishing the "Old Soldiers' Home." He argued the high number of Southerners who fought for the Union in the Civil War warranted the building of another facility in the South, and he believed the mountains of Tennessee provided a good climate for veterans, with consumption. Brownlow represented Tennessee's 1st District in the US House of Representatives from 1897 until his death in 1910. He also published the *Jonesboro Herald & Tribune* from 1876 to 1910. He was a nephew of Tennessee's radical post–Civil War governor, William "Parson" Brownlow. Congressman Brownlow died at the National Soldiers' Home on July 8 and is interred there. William Jennings Bryan, unsuccessful Democratic candidate for the presidency of the United States (1896, 1900, and 1908), spoke in Johnson City at the Hippodrome on February 21, 1911, to raise money for an obelisk monument for Brownlow. Tickets to the lecture, "The Price of a Soul," were 50¢ each. (Below, Frank Tannewitz Jr. collection.)

NOS. 1–2 BARRACKS. Residents, sometimes referred to as inmates, were initially admitted on a limited basis beginning on October 15, 1903. During the first year of operation, the home admitted only 363 veterans, 149 of them coming from Tennessee. The barracks in this postcard was one of several on the property with an initial capacity for up to 2,500 soldiers.

ROCK OUTCROPPING. This area is now forested and was dedicated as the Robert L. "Bob" Russell Rock Garden on June 4, 2000. A bronze plaque with the following inscription has been affixed to one of the rocks: "This tranquil site is named to honor Bob Russell for his many contributions to the Veterans Administration, James H. Quillen College of Medicine, Johnson City Medical Center, and the Johnson City Community Medical Center Director 1971 to 1981."

GENERAL MESS BUILDING. The dining hall (Building 34), one of the most beautiful of the original buildings, was designed by architect J.H. Freelander in the French Renaissance style of architecture. In what was known as the mess hall by the residents, tables were laid out with full table settings and good manners were expected from the residents. Staff members could eat at the facility and the "nickel plate" was only a nickel. The building also contains a clock tower that houses the original clockworks to this day. Today, the mess hall is home to the Museum at Mountain Home. The mission of the museum is to tell the story of the development of health care in South Central Appalachia from the earliest practitioner to the present.

CHAPEL. Robert Ripley featured the chapel (Building 13) in one of his *Believe It or Not* pieces because it accommodated both Catholic and Protestant services under one roof. The Protestant services were held in the east–west wing and the Catholic services were held in the north–south wing, with each church having its own altar, pipe organ, and decorations. The Catholic priest's home was located next door to the chapel. In the early days prior to the Catholic church having a full-time priest, the chapel's priest would also conduct services in town.

MEMORIAL HALL. The theater (Building 35), also called "the Opera House," was designed after the St. James Theater in New York City. In the early days, a wide variety of entertainment was hosted in this facility, including silent movies, light opera, and vaudeville. All residents were admitted free, and the family members of staff were admitted for a nickel.

HOSPITAL GROUP, NATIONAL SANATORIUM. Every room in the hospital had windows with a view of the grounds or the hospital's inner court. The inner court was beautifully landscaped with flowers and shrubs and furnished with park benches and a fountain to create a serene escape for mobile patients as well as staff.

POWERHOUSE, N.H.D.V.S. Prior to 1939, all the electricity used on the 447-acre property was produced in this building by a large generator and all the other utilities were provided in-house. The heat for all thirty-six buildings was generated with three 500-horsepower boilers and one 340-horsepower boiler pumping steam to the entire facility. The covered structure pictured at the east end of the building is where coal was stored for the boilers. The building was razed in the 1970s.

24

CARNEGIE LIBRARY. Congressman Brownlow wrote Andrew Carnegie and asked for a contribution to assist in building a library, which was not provided for in the initial funding. Carnegie responded with a short note and sent a check for $25,000, covering the entire cost of the project. Brownlow then wrote major publishers asking them to donate books. They responded with 16,000 volumes. The balcony of the library contained a section of children's books, which were used by the staff member's children, who sprawled out on the floor with them.

ADMINISTRATION BUILDING. Now part of the James H. Quillen College of Medicine, the building (52) renamed Ned R. McWherter Hall was one of the original structures at Mountain Home. It is located at the west end of Dogwood Avenue opposite the hospital complex, a little less than a half mile away at the east end of the street. Col. Lee Harr's office was on the third floor of this building during his long tenure as center director.

THE HOTEL AT SOLDIERS HOME. The hotel, razed sometime in the 1960s, provided accommodations for guests visiting loved ones but also contained a post exchange, post office, and a bowling alley/poolroom in the basement. Midcentury, the building housed a canteen with a manager's office on the ground floor, along with a hot snack kitchen and dining area where the vets could buy lunch until 4:30 p.m. In the basement were a barbershop, shoe repair shop, and post office.

BANDSTAND. Congressman Brownlow wrote the leading music companies and secured all the band instruments for the band. The band stayed busy during the summer, giving concerts on Monday, Wednesday, and Friday evenings at the bandstand, and on Sunday, it played under the trees in the afternoon and at the theater at night. It also played the musical score for silent movies at the Opera House on Tuesday and Thursday evenings. The raising and lowering of the flag between the bandstand and the mess hall was called the "flag up" and "flag down" ceremony.

LAKE BROWNLOW. The soldiers liked to fish in the pond, and for many years, area residents came to see and feed the swans. At night after closing, local kids would sneak into the facility to gig what were considered some of the biggest and best frogs in the area and, if caught, plead for mercy from Colonel Harr, who was considered a "very reasonable man."

"THE ENTIRE CEMETERY NOW HAS AROUND 3000 GRAVES." When graves were first installed at the Soldiers' Home, they were arranged in a circle, with Walter Brownlow's plot in the center of the circle. During this time, the cemetery was known as "the silent circle." In later years, as the cemetery grew, the graves were arranged in rows, which are typical in other national cemeteries.

"Soldier's Home Tenn." In the center of the photograph is the greenhouse, which was needed to support the extensive landscaping and formal flower gardens. Carl Anderson was the landscape architect responsible for the original landscape design for Mountain Home's grounds. He died on June 12, 1908, and is buried on the grounds in the "Special Section," which contains non-veteran individuals connected to Mountain Home.

Rose Circle. Located near the current location of Building 8, the rose circle was created by landscape artist Josh Gray. He also maintained the formal gardens where he mounted beds with cannas in the center, scarlet sage, ageratum, and dusty miller, making a red, white, and blue display. The image used for this postcard would have been made from the greenhouse area.

28

"DAIRY DEPT." As a self-sufficient facility, the Soldiers' Home ran its own farm and dairy, growing produce tended by able-bodied residents and managing a large herd of cows including purebred Jersey cows for dairy products and meat. The money earned by the "inmates" working the garden supplemented their pensions.

IN THE PARK. The Soldiers' Home zoo was home to this elk herd, as well as a bear, lions, deer, peacocks, coyotes, and a bald eagle, not to mention the numerous squirrels patrolling the grounds. The zoo provided another attraction for visitors to the grounds and a source of entertainment for the soldiers.

GUARD. There was a "member-guard" to enforce rules and regulations and a jail for confinement. The gates were locked at 9:00 p.m. and the trolley car to the home ended its run at that hour. In the beginning veterans were supplied surplus Civil War uniforms when they entered the home. "They drew two pairs of blue pants, two pairs of black shoes, four pairs of socks, three pairs of drawers, three shirts, a military dress blue coat, a pair of gloves, hat, cap, and suspenders." Discipline was strict, and the barracks were organized like the military (until World War II) with "companies" of men supervised by captains and sergeants. Full-time staff were given officers' ranks and wore uniforms.

NURSES MARCHING. The nurses in the 1939 Memorial Day parade are referred to as waitresses on this photograph. In the early days, nurses lived on the Soldiers' Home grounds in designated quarters and were required to be unmarried. Local nurses' training consisted of one year until 1921 when it was expanded to three years, but Soldiers' Home nurses were required to have a high school diploma and two years of training.

COL. LEE HARR PUBLIC ADDRESS SYSTEM. This late 1940s RPPC was taken during an address for a Memorial Day service. At the microphone is Col. Lee B. Harr, who was the longest-serving Medical Center director, from 1934 until 1966. On the far left is Chaplain Harry T. Wright, Mountain Home chaplain from 1946 to 1964, and to the right of the podium is B. Carol Reece, Republican representative for Tennessee's 1st Congressional District. Prior to working at Mountain Home, Col. Harr grew up and lived in a magnificent home at 300 West Watauga Avenue, where the Boxwood Terrace Professional Building is located today. His father, Isaac Harr, a prominent attorney, worked out of the Harr Building, located at 224½ East Main Street.

ELEANOR ROOSEVELT VISITS. Eleanor Roosevelt and an entourage that included Governor Cooper visited the Mountain Home Branch of the National Home for Disabled Soldiers on Memorial Day, May 30, 1939. A parade down Dogwood Avenue entertained the first lady and a crowd estimated at 25,000. The first lady also stopped in Johnson City at the old city hall auditorium located at the northwest corner of West Main and Boone Streets. At 8:00 p.m., she delivered a short speech titled "Problems of Youth."

Three

East Tennessee State University

VIEW OF CAMPUS OF EAST TENNESSEE STATE NORMAL SCHOOL. An early automobile is shown passing between the administration building later named Gilbreath Hall (right), for the school's first president, Sidney Gordon Gilbreath (serving 1910–1925), and the school's first library building, erected in 1922 (left). The library contained a 30-by-90-foot reading room, shelves for 10,000 books, an assembly room, classrooms, offices, and two small basement rooms. It was converted to a clinic when the first Sherrod Library was erected in 1931, and today, it houses the Reece Museum.

MAIN BUILDING. One of the original campus structures, Gilbreath Hall was first used to house the administrative offices and classrooms. Completed in 1910, the building is today home to the mathematics department, classrooms, and the Bud Frank Theater. Frank was director of theater for many years. East Tennessee State University (ETSU) is known as one of the most haunted campuses in the country due in part to stories of the spirit of "Uncle Sid," who died in 1961, turning off lights and closing open windows. Other buildings reported to be haunted include Burleson Hall and Clement Hall.

CARTER HALL. Another of the original campus buildings, it was named for Mayetta Wilkinson Carter, the wife of railroad magnate George L. Carter. During a tour of the Carter Addition in southwest Johnson City with Governor Patterson, Carter offered 120 acres of rolling land for the campus. After the tour, the group had lunch at the Soldiers' Home. The presence of the railroads and the Soldiers' Home were inextricably linked to the awarding of the school to Johnson City. Today, an updated but still charming Carter Hall continues to fulfill its original purpose as a residence hall for women.

PRESIDENT'S HOME. When the bids for the other original campus buildings came in under budget in early September 1910, it allowed President Gilbreath to add a president's home at a cost of $12,000. This house was razed for the construction of the D.P. Culp Center, which was completed in 1976. In 1972, the state purchased Shelbridge, built in 1921 by lumber dealer and mayor Roswell Spears, as the new home for the university president. Delos Poe Culp, the fourth president of ETSU (1968–1977), and his family moved into Shelbridge in the fall of 1973.

CAFETERIA. The dining hall was another of the original buildings on campus. In 1915, chef Hyder Bundy started his 40-plus year career preparing "the best food you'll ever eat, here or in heaven." For many of those years, he would ring an iron triangle dinner bell, summoning students to his latest feast. In the early years, gardens on the campus tended by students were used to stock the kitchen.

THE GYMNASIUM. Completed in 1922, ETSU's first gym contained a 50-by-70-foot playing room, two offices, basement showers, and seating to accommodate several hundred spectators. It was moved and converted for use by the Department of Music in 1955 and renamed Mathes Hall in memory of Charles Hodge Mathes who died on February 11, 1951. One of the original faculty members, Mathes served in various positions until his retirement in 1949.

COOPER HALL. The former home of George L. Carter, Cooper Hall became the school's second residence hall for women. The first house mother of Cooper was Ella V. Ross, a 1920 Science Hill graduate who later served as dean of women and dean of students from 1941 to 1972. Prior to being torn down in 1984, the structure was said to be haunted by Mayetta Carter, who died in 1957.

TRAINING SCHOOL. After visiting similar buildings at 40 teachers' colleges, President Sherrod planned many of the details of this building opened in 1929 as a training school for teachers. Over the years, many of its students were the children of faculty members. In 1968, it was named Alexander Hall for Phillip Wade Alexander, who came to serve as director of the training school in 1929. Alexander became dean of faculty in 1946 and served until 1958.

ENTRANCE TO EAST TENNESSEE STATE COLLEGE. The original campus globes mounted on brick columns grace the main entrances to ETSC. The globes were a gift from the class of 1945 and were dedicated on August 1, 1945. Four of the globes are currently located outside Gilbreath Hall, and two more are located at one of the campus entrances and two at the entrance to the amphitheater.

SCIENCE BUILDING. Dedicated on August 19, 1948, the college's new science building was touted to help train students for the "chemical age." It was later named D.M. Brown Hall for Dr. Dalton M. Brown, a graduate of Duke University who taught biology and botany classes during the 1930s and 1940s. Wings were added to the building, giving the facility its square configuration with its signature courtyard.

BROWNING HALL. Originally a residence purchased in 1949 and later enlarged and modernized, the structure was in disrepair when President Dossett took Gov. Gordon Browning (serving 1937–1939 and 1949–1953) on a tour of the campus. The president told the governor that the dorm was going to be named for him and the governor appropriated $500,000 in the state budget for renovations. Browning Hall stood where Sherrod Library is located today. The hall was home to many of the school's athletes from 1952 to 1973 during the time coach and physical education professor Loyd T. "Preacher" Roberts and his wife, Win, served as dorm parents.

MEMORIAL HALL. Now known as Brooks' Gym, it was named for J. Madison Brooks just prior to his retirement. The building served as the primary athletic facility from 1950 to 1977. In addition to athletic contests, the building housed physical education offices and classrooms and commencement exercises were held here until the opening of the "Mini-Dome" in the mid-1970s. The facility is currently home to the ETSU women's basketball and volleyball teams. Coach Brooks was recruited from Louisiana by Loyd T. Roberts to serve as head coach of the men's basketball team. His teams compiled 370 wins before his coaching career ended in 1973. Brooks remained as athletic director for seven more years.

AERIAL VIEW. The aerial view of the campus (above) was taken between 1962 and February 1963, when the school became a university. At that time, the enrollment was over 6,000 students, who came primarily from Eastern Tennessee, Virginia, and North Carolina. Memorial Stadium, a Works Progress Administration (WPA) project built from 1933 to 1935, is visible at the top center of the card. The stadium was used until its demolition in 1973 to build Memorial Center, better known as "the Mini-Dome," seen below about 12 years later. During that time, a number of new school facilities had been added, especially on the south end of the campus, to accommodate an increasing, more cosmopolitan student enrollment.

CHARLES C. SHERROD LIBRARY. Named for the second president of the college, Charles C. Sherrod (serving 1925–1949), the first Sherrod Library was constructed in 1931. When the new Sherrod Library was opened, the old building was renamed Nicks Hall in honor of eighth president Roy Nicks (1992–1996). Today, the building houses the Center for Appalachian Studies and Services.

AMPHITHEATER. Another WPA project completed in 1935, it has 14 tiers of grass seats for spectators around the stage. Located in the heart of the campus between the DP Culp Center and the old Sherrod Library/Nicks Hall, many campus events and performances have been held here over the years. Nicknamed the "passion pit," it has been a favorite spot of students and visitors since its completion.

DOSSETT DRIVE. This view to the northeast along Dossett Drive, named for Burgin E Dossett the third president of ETSU (serving 1949–1968), overlooks the state laboratory, planetarium, geology and geography building (now Hutcheson Hall, named in honor of Dr. R.H. Hutcheson, who served as Tennessee commissioner of public health from 1943 to 1975), and the health building (now Lamb Hall, named in honor of Dr. John P. Lamb Jr., first dean of ETSU's College of Health).

DORMITORIES. Pictured from left to right are Powell Hall, a men's dorm opened in 1961; Ross Panhellenic Hall, a women's dorm opened in 1965 and named in honor of Dean Ella Ross; and West Hall, a women's dorm opened in 1963.

PANORAMIC VIEW. This view overlooks Ross Drive; the university bookstore; business and educational building, erected in 1944 (now Sam Wilson Hall); and the University Center and grill, now called the Campus Center, which is home to, among other things, the George L. Carter Railroad Museum and the SUBmarine Gallery, an exhibition space for student art.

UNIVERSITY CENTER. Originally the Student Union Building, this structure designed by Johnson City architects Beeson & Beeson in the late 1950s opened in 1960 and housed a ballroom, faculty lounge, student offices, alumni office, cafeteria and grill, and a bowling alley in the basement where the George L. Carter Railroad Museum is located today.

Four

MILLIGAN COLLEGE

"MILLIGAN COLLEGE, NEAR JOHNSON CITY, TENN." Chartered as the Buffalo Male and Female Institute in 1866, it was changed to a four-year college in 1881 and renamed Milligan College. A liberal arts Christian college with about 1,200 students, its 235-acre campus overlooks Buffalo Mountain. It is regularly recognized as one of the best regional universities in the South.

MILLIGAN FROM A DISTANCE. In this c. 1917 image, the expanded classroom building (center) is visible. It was originally a two-room building completed in 1867, the cornerstone for an addition was laid on April 21, 1881. During his dedicatory speech, the same day, Josephus Hopwood (president from 1875 to 1903 and 1915 to 1917) announced the name of the institute was now Milligan College. In 1913, the original section of the Buffalo Institute was razed with a new larger section added. The expanded structure contained large classrooms, two society halls, a library, a bookstore, laboratories, and a new chapel with opera seats to hold 400 people. On November 16, 1918, while occupied by the Student Army Training Corps preparing men for service in World War I, the building caught fire and was lost.

MEE HALL. Mee Memorial Hall, opened in 1908, was named for Columbus A. and Francis T. Mee in 1910 when Francis donated the money to pay off the remaining debt. Mee Hall was a three-story, 32-room dorm located directly opposite the classroom building near the present site of the science building. It contained the campus dining room and kitchen and housed female students until 1913 when Hardin Hall opened. It was renovated in 1913 but burned down Christmas Eve 1915, leaving many of the male residents with nothing but the shirts on their backs. These young men found homes with local families, and a barracks was built for temporary housing.

ADMINISTRATION BUILDING. This structure, built in 1919, was named for Dr. Henry Derthick in 1978 after renovations were completed. Dr. Derthick served as president of Milligan for 23 years (1917 to 1940) when he and his wife, Perlea, retired. During that time, he had raised more than $3 million dollars and traveled more than 660,000 miles.

PARDEE HALL. This three-story, 70-room brick dorm, built by a Mr. Linville in 1919 and dedicated October 10, 1919, was designed by C.C. Mitchell of Johnson City. It was named in memory of Calvin Pardee, owner of the Cranberry Iron and Coal Company in Mitchell County, North Carolina. The building was torn down in 1992 due to disrepair.

GYMNASIUM. Cheek Hall, built in 1923–1924 and torn down in 1979, was named in honor of Joel O. Cheek, developer of Maxwell House Coffee and a Milligan trustee that donated more than $100,000 to the school. Constructed of brick, it seated 900 people and was considered one of the finest gyms in the region—much better than the one at East Tennessee State.

48

BUFFALO CREEK AND GARDEN SCENE. A dam on Buffalo Creek, water wheel fish pond, and lily pool were constructed during the "Milligan the Beautiful Campaign" promoted by Perlea Derthick in 1930. Steps leading down to the creek were built in the teens. The steps contain the dates of American wars through the Civil War and the names of presidents, ending with Woodrow Wilson. In addition to students, local families would come to the campus for a picnic or a stroll on the beautifully landscaped campus, one of the most attractive spots in the region.

SCENE ON MILLIGAN COLLEGE CAMPUS. Hardin Hall (foreground) and Pardee Hall (back, right) are pictured in this Cline postcard. Hardin Hall is named for George W. Hardin, a member of the first graduating class at Milligan and likely on the school's first baseball team. He was "a constant attendant at the baseball games" and was considered one of the best "fans" in the bleachers. In tears, he convinced the Derthicks to stay at Milligan after their initial visit went poorly. His ability to raise large sums of money, including his own donations, made him a major benefactor of the school. He started as a switchman with ET&WNC Railroad in 1886 and worked his way up to supervise the entire system as vice president and general manager.

SUTTON HALL AND WEBB HALL. Sutton Hall was dedicated in 1956 and named for Webb and Nanye Bishop Sutton. Webb was the president of Sutton Construction Company in Richmond, Virginia. Nanye, from Snowville, Virginia, was one of the 22-member Milligan class of 1900. After Webb's death, his wife donated the funds for the construction of Webb Hall in his memory. It was completed in 1960 with the capacity to accommodate 170 residents. Stahl Hall, the former home of Ray Stahl, prior to its use as a residence hall, was razed to make way for Webb Hall.

Hart Hall - Dormitory for 188 Women.

HART HALL. The largest residence hall, located across the street from the McCormick Dining Center, was completed in 1965 to accommodate 180 women. Dr. John Hart and his wife, Pearl Hart, donated the funds for the project in memory of his parents Charles Bissell and Tecora Billingsley Hart. In 1985, Dr. Hart's sister Cleo Hart McMahan donated $500,000 to Milligan, her alma mater, to build the John E. McMahan Student Union Building in memory of her husband.

The P. H. Welshimer Memorial Library.

P.H. WELSHIMER MEMORIAL LIBRARY. Pearl Howard Welshimer was a Restoration Movement (which sought "the unification of all Christians in a single body patterned after the church of the New Testament") leader and father of Mildred Welshimer Phillips, who joined the Milligan faculty in 1947, serving as dean of women. The library opened in 1961 and was necessitated in part by Mildred's gift of her deceased sister's personal library of 7,000 volumes.

Five

STREET SCENES

VIEW FROM ROAN HILL. This early view from Roan Hill overlooks the Tree Streets area toward downtown. In the distance is Tannery Knob, visible on the right half of the picture. The First Christian Church is visible, almost centered on the high point of Tannery Knob, and the old pre-1910 Science Hill High School is visible in the far left center of the image. The rounded Munsey Church building does not appear to be present, dating the photograph to pre-1908.

BIRD'S-EYE VIEW. In 1900, Johnson City was a small town under 5,000 inhabitants but nearly doubled by 1910 after the development of the Soldiers' Home and award of the normal school. The postcard above, produced by John D. Longmire, dates to the early 1900s when the city was in the midst of this growth spurt that would continue until the 1930s. Longmire had a confectionary store at 101 East Main Street. This view looks south from Tannery Knob along Division Street with the Carlisle Hotel sitting in the foreground, and the smokestack (right) likely belongs to the American Cigar Box Lumber Company at the intersection of Division and Walnut Streets. Heavy smoke visible at the far left of the image belongs to the Harris Manufacturing Company. The postcard below dates to the 1920s, and the view looks toward downtown along South West Avenue toward the Model Mill and the Tree Streets.

54

HIGH WATER. May 29, 1908, was a memorable day in Johnson City for all the wrong reasons. Brush Creek swollen from heavy rains escaped its banks and flooded the downtown, something that has been a semi-regular occurrence for many years. This view from Science Hill shows the expansiveness of the flood. In 2014, the city constructed its first floodwater mitigation park, Founders Park, and a second King Commons, opened in 2017 to alleviate flooding. (Frank Tannewitz Jr. collection.)

SPRING STREET. This early-1900s image, taken just north of the intersection of Spring and Tipton Streets, looks northwest toward Main Street and the Unaka National Bank (Freiberg's Restaurant today). The building on the corner (right) housed the City Drug Company and would be razed for the erection of the Unaka and City (later Hamilton) National Bank Building.

WATAUGA AVENUE. Some of the finest homes in the city were located along Watauga Avenue in the late-19th and early-20th centuries, so it is not surprising it was one of seventeen streets to be served by the Johnson City & Carnegie Street Railroad Company (JC&C), which ran its first 24-foot passenger car on August 29, 1891. The depression of the early 1890s doomed this incarnation of the trolley line, with the last car running December 1, 1894. The line saw some revival in 1896, with summer excursion trips to Lake Watausee until 1900, when the tracks were removed. However, the award of the Soldiers' Home revived interest in the line, so the owners of the JC&C reorganized as the Johnson City Traction Company and had track laid to the new Soldiers' Home in July 1903, with more than five miles of track extending through other parts of the city a year later. Development of the motor bus killed the use of trolleys in the United States, and the city's last streetcar ran in 1932.

MARKET STREET. The old Civil War–era Stage Road became Market Street as the settlement along Brush Creek transformed into Johnson City. This March 11, 1909, postcard view looking east along East Market Street at the corner of Roan contains an early image of Munsey Memorial Methodist Episcopal Church building, erected in 1908. Also visible at 203 and 205 Market Street are the new parsonage for Rev. S.B. Vaught built in 1907, and the home of Dr. CJ Broyles, respectively.

MEMPHIS TO BRISTOL HIGHWAY. The 538-mile Memphis-to-Bristol Highway was also known as State Route 1 and, later, as Tennessee's portion of the "Broadway of America." In 1911, the Commercial Club, the forerunner of the chamber of commerce, created a highway association to advocate for the proposed highway to run through Johnson City. Eventually, it did in later years via US Route 11E (West Market Street).

MAIN STREET, THE 1900S. The view in the image above looks east, and that in the image below looks west along Main Street. Both were taken prior to the streets being paved in 1908 and after 1903–1904, when tracks for the trolley were laid. The above view appears to be earlier, with numerous large power poles and the overhead trolley wire visible. Below, a few power poles are visible, and the street appears muddy in places along the tracks. At some point, between the above and below photographs being taken, the large power poles were replaced with fewer short power poles to supply electricity for the trolley as well as lighting. In the west view, a restaurant and home with trees sitting behind them along Brush Creek are visible at the future location of the Pardue/Windsor Hotel.

MAIN STREET, 1910S. The east (above) view published by the Bee Hive dates to 1910–1911, just prior to Summers-Parrott Hardware (104–106, second building on the right) moving to their new location on Buffalo Street. The third building on the right at the corner of Spring Street is Gump Brothers (108–110), which sold men's clothing in this location from about 1880 to 1921. The west (below) view was taken at the corner of Roan and Main Streets. Wofford Brothers Insurance at 253 was founded in the late 1800s and operates today as Johnson City Wofford Bros. Insurance. Next door at 251 with the clock in front on the street is the William Silver Company, jewelers and opticians, then the Kress and Majestic Theater a little farther along. On the opposite side of the street, at 248, is a tooth sign for dentist J.P. Metzger, located in the Burrows Building, and beyond that are the Edisonia Theater and Dosser Brothers. Both views show paved streets with fewer power poles visible.

MAIN STREET, LOOKING WEST, JOHNSON CITY, TENN.

MAIN STREET, 1920S. The east view (above), published by the Asheville Postcard Company, dates to about 1921 when the Unaka and City National Bank moved into the six-story structure on the southeast corner of Main and Spring Streets. On the southwest corner sits the Tennessee National Bank in the old Gump Brothers location. This structure was erected in 1914. On the opposite side of the street are the Savoy Drug Company at 201 Main Street; H.E. Hart at 203, jeweler and watchmaker; Faw & DeVault, selling dry goods, clothing, and shoes at 205 in the old Bee Hive location; and just beyond that, at 213, Hannah's (Atomik Comics today). The west view (below), taken from Roan Street, clearly shows the Majestic marquee billing Ernest Truex in *Six Cylinder Love*, the film debut of Thomas Mitchell, released November 4, 1923. Woolworth's is located in the old William Silver Company building, and the Hotel Windsor sign is clearly visible at the far end of the street.

60

MAIN STREET, THE 1930S–1950S. From 1930 to 1960, Johnson City's population only increased by about 6,000 souls to 31,000, but many consider this the downtown's golden age. Main Street was the heart of the city's prosperous retail business district of over 384 storefronts, which handled over $40 million in sales annually, serving a four-state area during this time. The iconic view above, looking east toward the square, is a commonly found postcard image. It features vintage signage for Parks-Belk, the Mecca Restaurant, Royal Crown Cola, and Boston Shoe Shop. Today, one of downtown's long-lived businesses, Mel's Stamps & Coins, at 85 Buffalo Street is in the same location as the Mecca. The view below has signage for longtime anchor businesses, including Penney's (moved to this modern-looking storefront at 307–313 Main Street in 1948), Kress, and King's department stores.

LOOKING EAST ON MAIN STREET, 1931. Serendipitously, *Street Scene* (released September 5, 1931) starring Sylvia Sidney and Beulah Bondi in her debut, headlines the Majestic marquee at 239 East Main Street. The 880-seat Majestic opened as a vaudeville theater in 1902 before becoming a motion picture theater in the 1920s when owners installed a $20,000 pipe organ and a climate control system that made the theater "the coolest place in town" to catch a movie.

The Kress sits just beyond the Majestic on the same side of the road, and just across the street, at 236 Main Street, is the Criterion Theater with its large neon sign brought from the Criterion in Atlanta in the 1920s. The Criterion started out as the Edisonia about 1909, but when it closed its doors about 1937, it was called the State. At 232 Main Street is I.N. Beckner's Sons, a jeweler and watchmaker doing business in town from 1886 until it closed in late 1985.

LOOKING WEST ON MAIN STREET, 1940S. The Majestic marquee advertises "Its Gable & Garson in Fleming's Exciting *Adventure*." *Adventure* premiered December 28, 1945. Just beyond, on the same side of the street, is the Liberty Theater sign at 221 East Main Street. The Liberty was the smallest of the downtown theaters and the place to go for western B movies. On the (left) corner of Main and Roan Streets at 246 East Main in the c. 1900 Burrows Building is Masengill's, a department store known for formal men's and women's clothing and bridal

wear. John Masengill opened the store in November 1916 and owned it until his death. It was purchased by Ambers Wilson in 1958, but the doors recently closed for good in February 2018 when furnishings accumulated over 100 years were sold at auction. On the opposite corner in the 1907 King Building is Liggett's Drug Store (257 Main Street), one of the most popular and longest-lasting downtown drugstores.

AERIAL VIEW, 1960S, AND MAIN STREET, 1970S. The landmark Giant Food/U-Haul sign (in white) is visible at the left center of the above card. The tall sign dates to the construction and grand opening of the Little Food Stores new "super market" on January 19, 1956. In 1959, the name of Commerce Street store was changed to Giant Food Market. This landmark sign was recently refurbished by the city with the shape inspired by historic railroad signs and a tri-star element representing Tennessee's three regions. The work was part of the $2.9 million King Commons floodwater mitigation project to alleviate flooding. The image on the card below was taken in the 1970s, the beginning of the downtown's decline resulting from retail businesses relocating to the new retail district tied to construction of the "Miracle Mall" at the north end of town about 1971.

Six

AT WORK

CRANBERRY FURNACE. Originally named the Carnegie Furnace, it processed iron ore brought in on the narrow-gauge railroad from Cranberry, North Carolina. Built in 1890 by Harry Hargraves, who was hired from Alabama, the new furnace was constructed just east of the Carnegie Addition, two miles from downtown Johnson City. Hundreds of Italian immigrant and black workers were hired to build the furnace. There were so many Italians coming in by train every day that the *Comet* noted that "in a few weeks a stranger coming to Johnson City will think he is in Italy." When finished, the furnace was believed to be the second Bessemer-type blast furnace constructed in Tennessee (behind Chattanooga in 1887) and potentially in the entire South.

"SCENE NEAR JOHNSON CITY, TENN." Although rail brought industry to Johnson City, it also expanded the markets that could be reached for the fertile farmlands and agriculture nearby. The Johnson City Commercial Club touted the area as having the finest clover, alfalfa, and other grasses for grazing and claimed that "this city will soon be the distributing center for the largest apple shipments in the world."

STEAM DONKEY. A steam donkey is a steam-powered winch invented in 1881 by John Dolbeer that revolutionized 19th-century logging operations in areas with difficult or steep terrain and large logs beyond the capability of a team of oxen or horses. The operator was referred to as a donkey puncher. This postcard was postmarked 1908 in Johnson City and mailed to Polly Dunn in Vaughtsville, Johnson County, Tennessee. At that time, there were 8 lumber wholesalers and 12 lumber manufacturers listed in the city directory.

MODEL FLOUR MILL. The Model Mill at 500 West Walnut Street was built by George L. Carter in 1909, with an opening day of Saturday, March 19, 1910. Upon opening, mill leadership consisted of J.W. Ring, president; J. H. Bates, head miller; J.T. Miller, head millwright, and S.A. Burnett, second miller. The mill's initial daily capacity was 1,000 barrels of flour, 3,000 bushels of meal, and 100,000 pounds of feed. It produced 94 percent bran-free flour under the old trade name Red Band. In 1933, General Mills Inc. acquired it for a million dollars and operated the facility until 2003, when the plant closed. In 2016, R&G Ventures, owned by Grant Summers, the president of Summers-Taylor Inc., bought the property for renovation as Summers-Taylor's corporate headquarters as well as for several other tenants, including ETSU.

SUMMERS HARDWARE. Summers has been providing hardware to Johnson Citians for more than 125 years. In 1888, Joseph P. Summers bought a half interest in a hardware store started by G.C. Seavers, which became Seavers & Summers. In 1893, James A. Summers partnered with his uncle Ben D. Lyle to acquire the business, which became Summers & Lyle. After a number of partnership and name changes, a switch to wholesale after 1910, moving to its present location at 400 Buffalo Street, and reorganizing after the Great Depression, the company has evolved into the leading industrial distributor in East Tennessee.

LOVE-THOMAS COMPANY. Located at the corner of Ashe and Earnest Streets, the Love-Thomas Company was a successful wholesale dry goods and notions business established in January 1907. It employed six traveling salesmen who covered a five-state area. By 1914, the building was being used by the Carolina, Clinchfield & Ohio Railway (CC&O) for its offices.

THE BEE HIVE. The Bee Hive department store, located between East Main and Market Streets at 207–209 East Main, opened in 1890 and sold dry goods, millinery, men's and women's wear, groceries, hardware, stationery (including postcards), wallpaper, drugs, and sundries. The proprietors were Philo M. Ward and C.D. Friberg, who oversaw 20 employees. The store closed about 1920, and the building saw other department stores follow, with Parks-Belk located there for many years.

KRESS. Samuel H. Kress started a chain of 5¢, 10¢, and 25¢ department stores in 1896 and "envisioned his stores as works of art that would contribute to the cityscape." In 1910, Kress built a unique brick building at 243 East Main Street that was extensively remodeled in 1963. Kress sold "just about everything," including its own line of postcards, and had a lunch and candy counter. Today, the building is the corporate headquarters for Allied Dispatch.

UNAKA AND CITY NATIONAL BANK. JOHNSON CITY, TENN. 107422

WHITEHOUSE DRUG CO. Downtown Johnson City has been home to numerous pharmacies over the years. Most of them had lunch counters and a soda fountain where customers could sit and eat a delicious meal while shopping for typical sundries or picking up medicine. Harry Whitehouse opened his namesake drugstore, located at 211 East Main Street (current location of Holy Taco and Cantina), in 1909 after running a similar endeavor for three years in Knoxville.

UNAKA & CITY NATIONAL BANK. This six-story structure, erected in 1921 at 200–202 East Main Street, was the home of the Unaka & City National Bank created when the Unaka National and City National Banks merged on September 11, 1920. At the time of the merger, the Unaka Bank was worth $38,500. Twelve years later, the conglomerate was then taken over by Hamilton National Bank on September 30, 1932. The Hamilton Bank was renamed Suntrust Bank and moved to 207 Mockingbird Lane on October 6, 1995.

72

EDISONIA. When the Edisonia opened its doors as a vaudeville theater around 1908, it was located at 248 East Main Street and the proprietors were Smith & Nitram. By 1913, ownership had changed, along with the location, to 236 East Main Street in a building that dates to 1904. This building is the only surviving structure to house one of the original downtown theaters. In this postcard, signs for three of the four westerns advertised can be seen. They are *A Sonata of Souls*, *Shifty's Claim*, and *A Desperado*—all three released between April and May 1911. One of the signs reads, "POSITIVELY no tickets sold on credit."

JOHNSON CITY HIGH SCHOOL. The Science Hill Male and Female Institute, founded on October 27, 1867, opened for school on August 24, 1868, in a newly constructed building (above) that was used until the second, larger version (below) was built. The first building was razed in 1910, and the new building erected on what students referred to as "the Hill." This new, modern facility, designed by prominent architect Albert B. Baumann (1861–1942) of Bauman and Bauman in Knoxville, Tennessee, was opened later in 1910. This structure was a central part of downtown and fondly remembered by students. After the high school moved to the new facility on John Exum Parkway March 6, 1961, the building later housed South Junior High School.

SCIENCE HILL. From 1910 to 1962, students ascended 88 steps to this temple of learning. Twice each school day, the ROTC cadets carried out a formal ceremony at the flagpole, raising the flag in the morning and lowering it in the afternoon. Students and folks passing by stopped to pay their respects to the flag. The arrowhead-shaped monument (lower left) was thought to have been erected by Joseph Hampton Rich in 1929 to commemorate the Daniel Boone Trail. The monument was torn down on April 9, 1979, but the original bronze tablet was saved and the monument rebuilt on the Munsey Memorial United Methodist Church grounds and rededicated in June 2006 by the John Sevier Chapter, Daughters of the American Revolution.

LANGSTON HIGH SCHOOL. Located at the corner of Myrtle Avenue and Elm Street, Langston was one of three schools, along with Martha Wilder and Columbus Powell, planned in 1892. What set it apart was its designation for black students, thanks to the efforts of Dr. Hezekiah Hankal, a black physician, teacher, and preacher, making it the first black public high school. Named for Mercer Langston, the first black elected to public office in the United States, the school's motto was "Enter to Learn. Depart to Serve."

MARTHA WILDER SCHOOL. Though the name is misprinted on this postcard, the school was named for the wife of Gen. John T. Wilder, who gave the land for the school. Built in 1893 at the corner of New Street and Myrtle Avenue for students living in the northern part of town, the school cost $10,000, about $2,500 more than Columbus Powell, which was built at the same time for students living in the eastern part of the city. S.A. Crockett was the first principal of the school.

WEST SIDE SCHOOL. This school, built in 1907, was located where the Watauga Square Apartments sit today at 503 West Watauga Avenue near the intersection with West Main Street. The school was torn down in 1961, but the school's retaining wall and steps remain.

JOHNSON CITY BUSINESS COLLEGE, 1936. In 1935, the college, located in the Johnson City Press Building at 204 Main Street, advertised that it had been in continuous operation for over 25 years. In the early years of the school, the college was located at 121½ Spring Street. Pictured are 192 students and 7 faculty members. The faculty member left of center is C.E. Rogers, who served as Johnson City school superintendent, and the man in the center is the president of the school, I.R. Thornberry.

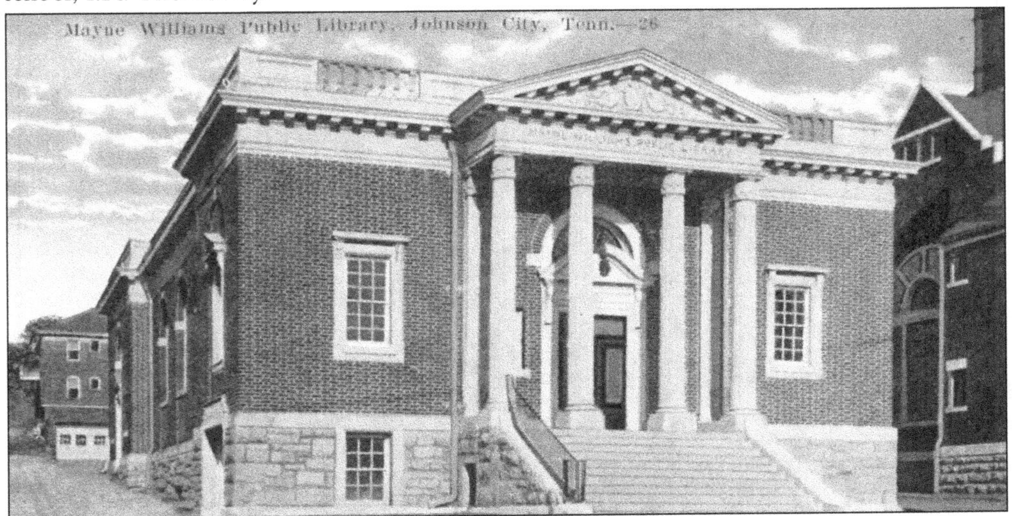

MAYNE WILLIAMS PUBLIC LIBRARY. The Mayne Williams Public Library, located at 205 South Roan Street, opened to the public on January 1, 1923. Samuel Cole Williams, a Johnson City judge and historian who was appointed to the Tennessee Supreme Court, donated a parcel of land on Roan Street and $10,000 toward its construction in memory of his young son, Mayne Williams, who died July 30, 1897, just short of his fourth birthday after innocently ingesting sugarcoated quinine pills.

MUNICIPAL BUILDING. Completed in 1920 at the corner of Boone and Market Streets, this structure was the first city-owned building to house city offices and business. Folks with their children lined up on both sides of this building in July 1957 to receive the new polio vaccine. The building was razed, and the property is now part of the Johnson City Press complex.

MEMORIAL HOSPITAL. Formerly the home of Cy Lyle, publisher of the *Comet*, this two-story, 16-room brick house at 809 Seventh (Chilhowie) Avenue was the second home of the hospital, from 1915 to 1921. Earlier, the hospital had opened its doors to the public on May 10, 1911. In 1921, the hospital moved to a new, larger facility and its name was changed to Appalachian Hospital.

APPALACHIAN HOSPITAL. Located at the corner of Boone Street and Fairview Avenue, the Appalachian Hospital and School of Nursing (above) opened in 1921. The building cost $100,000, half of which was borrowed through the Hospital Corporation, a group of 11 doctors who practiced in the hospital. A charter for a new corporate hospital was received on April 12, 1945, and excluded ownership by the doctors and dentists. Ground was broken on July 14, 1949, for a renovation of the old hospital and construction of a new facility next to it. The first patient was admitted to the new Memorial Hospital (below) on February 15, 1951. This site operated until Labor Day, September 1, 1980, when 154 patients were transferred from Memorial Hospital to the new Johnson City Medical Center.

POST OFFICE AND FEDERAL BUILDING. Erected in 1910 and located at the corner of Ashe and West Walnut Streets, this was the first federally owned building in Johnson City (above). Federal authorities told George L. Carter that they would award the contract to the group that built the sidewalks for the structure. Carter donated the land and had sidewalks built overnight to secure the location near his Model Mill and Southwest Addition. Afterward, the building was used as a courthouse and for Washington County 911 operations. In March 1938, the post office moved from its Ashe Street location to the new $197,000 white marble building at 338 East Main Street (below), where WJHL's television station is currently located. The post office moved to 530 East Main Street in the summer of 1974.

TRI-CITY AIRPORT. With Sen. Kenneth McKellar championing commercial aviation projects like this in Tennessee, the Works Progress Administration (WPA) provided over $1,000,000 for construction of the Tri-City Airport, which opened on September 1, 1937. The airport saw its first airliner, an American Airlines DC-2, on November 5, 1937, the same day the facility was dedicated, with the field being named for Senator McKellar. The airport, located between each of the Tri-Cities in Blountville, has grown from 323 acres to 1,260 acres and now serves over 200,000 passengers a year.

TIPTOP RESTAURANT. This RPPC dates to May 1904. The owner, George R. Brown, in the apron, stands next to his wife, Sallie, and their two children Melvin (with *Cincinnati Post* newspapers in hand) and Phoebe in front of them. The Tiptop restaurant, located at the corner of Tipton and Buffalo Streets, also provided lodging for 25¢ until closing in 1908. The advent of the railroad allowed items like fresh oysters to be enjoyed by the previously isolated population.

THE SPOT STEAK HOUSE. Formerly named the Roxy, with the slogan "the students rendezvous spot," this restaurant became the Spot Steak House. It was located at 421 East Main Street about where the McDonald's is today. The Spot, fondly remembered for its special steaks and other fine food, was owned by Don F. and G.W. "Bill" Bradford, who bred their own Aberdeen Angus cattle.

THE PRIDE OF EAST TENNESSEE. Originally known as the Dixie Bar-B-Q, the Dixie Restaurant, owned by George and Mary Parker, opened on September 30, 1930, at 425 East Main Street and closed in 1972 after 42 years of dishing up mouthwatering food. The Parkers pioneered curb service in Johnson City.

82

Seven

HOTELS AND HOMES

THE CARNEGIE HOTEL. The Carnegie Addition, located northeast of Johnson City, was planned and implemented by the Carnegie Land and Improvement Company led by famed Civil War general John T. Wilder. The lavish 125-room Carnegie Hotel, built in 1891 at the southwest corner of Broadway and Second (Fairview) Avenue for $125,000, was but one of the many features planned for this development, but much of it was never realized due to the Panic of 1893. The hotel burned to the ground April 3, 1910. (Frank Tannewitz Jr. collection.)

PARDUE AND WINDSOR HOTEL. The 50-room Hotel Pardue, built in 1909 by Henry Wilson Pardue, was located at 101–103 West Main Street prior to being demolished in the summer of 1971. The three-story brick building was across the street from Fountain Square and convenient to nearby passenger railway stations. Sometime during 1913, the ownership changed along with the name. The newly christened Windsor Hotel, sometimes known as Hotel Windsor, was run by William F. Green and his wife, Reba. They were also the proprietors of the Pineola Inn in North Carolina and offered two-day excursion trips by rail for $5 a person that covered fare, meals, and room. The business was so successful that by 1917 through the mid-1920s, they annexed the Arlington Hotel for additional rooms and referred to the business as the Windsor Hotel & Annex. By 1935, James H. Preas Jr. and his brother Ralph A. Preas were proprietors.

THINK! This postcard add for the Windsor Hotel and Annex may have been provided as a courtesy to guests. The 1920 Sanborn map shows the Windsor Annex in the same location as the Arlington Hotel, and the 1919 city directory indicates Reba L. Green was the proprietor after the passing of her husband. The 65 rooms with running water were rented at $1, and there was a 50¢ upcharge if one had a bath in the room; for another half dollar, one could get a meal.

ARLINGTON HOTEL. Located on Fountain Square across West Main Street from the Pardue/ Windsor Hotel, the Arlington Hotel was part of the vibrant downtown during its heyday. It was built on the original property of Henry Johnson, who built the Hoss House on this same location in 1871. Johnson's brother-in-law Elkanah Hoss ran the Hoss House after Henry's death. The Arlington Hotel building was demolished in the summer of 1971, about the same time as the Windsor.

COLONIAL HOTEL. When the three-story Colonial Hotel with its six stately columns opened July 15,1909, to the traveling public, it was considered a most modern accommodation with electric lights, steam heat, private baths, as well as each bedroom supplied with hot and cold running water and phones. Located at 215 East Market Street, it was two blocks from the depot but close to the business center of town. All 60 rooms were outside rooms with fire escapes and standpipes on each floor, and its 190 feet of veranda space provided "one of the grandest views of the mountains in the city." N.L. Murrell was the proprietor and manager of the Colonial when it opened. He was well known in hostelry circles as the proprietor of General Wilder's Cloudland Hotel on top of Roan Mountain and for building the Lynwood in Elizabethton. The Colonial was razed in the 1960s for parking at Munsey Memorial Methodist Church.

JOHN SEVIER HOTEL. The 10-story John Sevier Hotel opened on August 5, 1924, at 204 South Roan Street adjacent to the Southern Depot on the former site of the old Faw home and Boxwood Inn. When it opened, it was called the social and business headquarters of the "State of Appalachia" and was a "beehive" of activity in the center of town for many years. The above postcard depicts the first phase and the below postcard image was captured after the second phase was completed in the late 1920s. It was designed by local architect D.R. Beeson and cost $150,000. A planned third phase fell victim to the Great Depression and was never built. Many of the stories of Al Capone visiting Johnson City involve the John Sevier, including one in which Capone rented the entire third floor. Today, the John Sevier Center is a low-income housing facility, but it still stands tall in downtown and in the memories of longtime residents.

MONTROSE COURT. Located today at 701 West Locust Street in what was referred to as the Southwest (Carter) Addition, this 28-unit Tudor-style structure was designed by D.R. Beeson Sr. and built in 1922. It featured 6 five-room apartments, 11 four-room apartments, 5 three-room apartments, and 2 one-room apartments. The building burned down on November 13, 1928, but was rebuilt. It is one of three locations commonly associated with Al Capone. Numerous anecdotal stories abound that he visited Johnson City, dubbed the "Little Chicago of the South," as he traveled between Chicago and Miami during Prohibition.

"Melubro Court"

MELUBRO COURT. Built in 1912 on the northwest corner of North Roan and 101 East Watauga Avenue, this structure was renovated in 2013. At one time, it was the home of Johnson City native Gwen Terasaki, the author of the book *Bridge to the Sun.* Published in 1957, the book recounts the family's experiences before, during, and after World War II. It was made into a film that premiered in Johnson City in 1961.

"Heller Apartments"

HELLER APARTMENTS. Located at 112 West Unaka Boulevard, this 1928 apartment building was also known as the Maple Terrace Apartments. Originally constructed with eight apartments, it was one of 45 apartment houses in the city. It was remodeled in 2012.

BOARDING HOME. Boardinghouses provided food and lodging for paying guests and were a sought-after commodity for those seeking affordable lodging, short- or long-term, during the first half of the 20th century. This RPPC postmarked March 12, 1907, has a message that the sender had dinner at this place. The 1908 city directory indicates there were eight boardinghouses in the city.

WESTOVER MANOR. This postcard dated 1954 was sent by a tourist who thought this was a really nice place to stay. The Westover was located at 244 Old Jonesboro Road (2810 West Walnut today) near the Cherokee Golf Course. Operated by Margaret E. and George Hannah, it was advertised as a high-class, modern, private home "known from coast to coast." At one point, it was used as a fraternity house and was razed after a fire sometime in the 1980s.

UNAKA TOURIST HOME. Sophia Templin was hostess of this house located at 102 East Unaka Avenue. Its slogans were "Just one door away from the Highway-11E, 19W, 23" and "Look for the Black & White Sign." Sophia's husband, Hubert, a pharmacist, worked at the Snyder-Jones Pharmacy and operated the Super Laboratory, a medicine manufacturer.

BROADWAY CAMP AND BEVERLY COURT. Originally called Marion's Camp, it was purchased by Robert Johnson prior to World War II and was renamed Broadway Camp (above) before Johnson sold it to Cecil Crowe, who renamed it Broadway Court. After the war, Johnson built a new 25-unit motel about a mile north of town (today near Roan and Sunset), taking the name Beverly from Beverly Hills. Beverly Court (below) offered tub and shower, radios, fans, steam and electric heat, and a coffee shop. Ed and Lexie Leonard Reedy, the last of the three owners, sold it to First Federal so they could retire. First Federal had the structure demolished in September 1964 to build one of its branches there.

THE PIONEER. The Pioneer was located two and a half miles north of Johnson City at the intersection of Highways 11E, 19, 23, and 411, about where Johnson City Honda is located today at 2806 North Roan Street. I.W. Garland and H.C. Seaton were proprietors at one time. It grew from 22 units to 45 units with steam heat, a private tiled bath, radio, television, and Beautyrest mattresses.

SILVER LEAF TOURIST COURT. Located one mile east of town on US Route 11E, the hotel offered modern, clean, comfortable accommodations for the traveler. It was owned by Bill and Lorene Cure. The restaurant was known for its chicken in a basket.

RIO MOTEL. Owned and operated by Mamie and George G. Runyon, the Rio boasted wall-to-wall carpeting, free TV, telephones in the room, ceramic-tile baths, air-conditioning, a coffee shop, a swimming pool, and a children's playground. This "ultra-modern" motel was located on US Routes 11E, 19, 23, and 411, with the current address of 2106 North Roan Street. The building has been repurposed as Paul's Mall, a mini strip mall next to the Parkway Center.

INNS OF AMERICA OF JOHNSON CITY. Built in the early 1960s at 106 West Millard Street (now the library parking lot), it boasted gracious living in the heart of the city with 112 modern units each equipped with air-conditioning, two telephones, free television, radio, and Muzak. Guests enjoyed the panoramic view from the swimming pool in the sky (on the roof) and could dine at the Americana Restaurant. In later years, before it was torn down, residents referred to the inn as "Sins of America," due to questionable clientele.

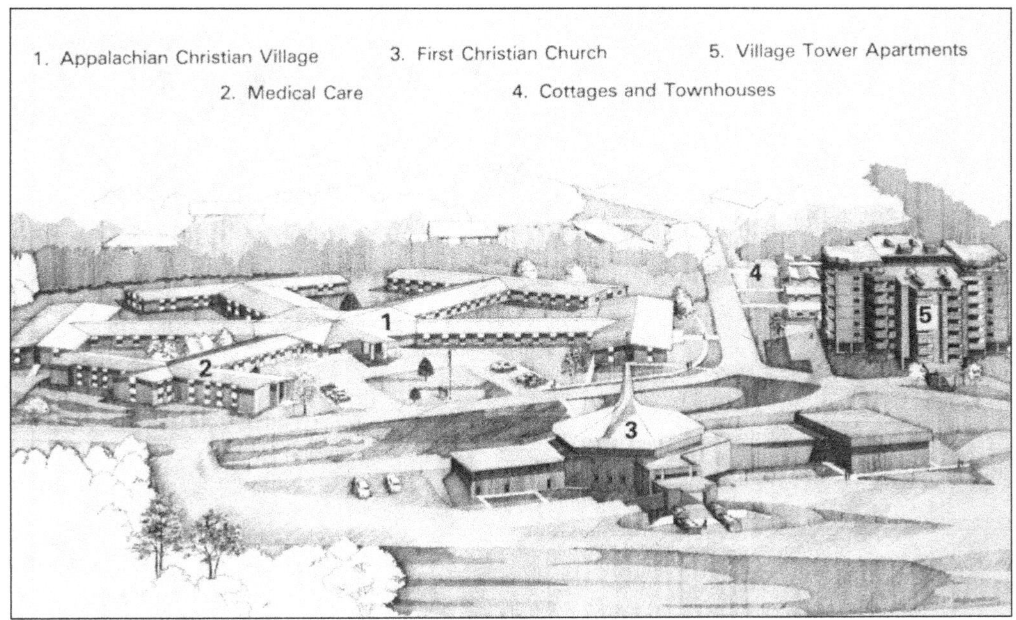

APPALACHIAN CHRISTIAN VILLAGE. This retirement village is the fulfillment of Dr. Joseph Dampier's vision in 1951 to honor the biblical challenges regarding the aged (Matthew 25 and Isaiah 46). Dr. Dampier, as minister of First Christian Church of Johnson City, encouraged his congregation and area churches to support this vision. The complex, now called Cornerstone Village, was built in 1966 with a nursing facility and a condo-based retirement home and is located at 2012 Sherwood Drive.

ROBIN'S ROOST. Located at 1309 South Roan Street, this home was built about 1890 and was purchased in 1892 by Robert L. "Our Bob" Taylor who lived in the home five years. The home's name came from Taylor inviting friends to the house saying, "Let's go where the robins roost," owing to swarms of robins gathered there. His brother, Alfred A. "Alf" Taylor, lived in the home from 1900 until 1903. Bob, a Democrat, and Alf, a Republican, squared off in the 1886 gubernatorial campaign dubbed "War of the Roses." Bob's supporters wore white roses and Alf's sported red roses. Unlike earlier (and current) campaigns, the "war" featured good-natured storytelling, fiddle playing, and practical jokes. Bob won, but Alf got his turn when elected governor of Tennessee in 1920. After Alf left the home, W.E. Burbage, secretary of the Watauga Water Company, lived there.

BIRTHPLACE OF SEN. ROBERT L. TAYLOR. Robert Love Taylor, a three-term Tennessee governor and one-term US senator, was born in this home in Happy Valley on July 31, 1850. He was a charismatic speaker, and politics flowed through his veins; his father was Nathaniel Greene Taylor, a farmer and Methodist minister who lost a congressional race to Andrew Johnson, and his maternal uncle was Landon Carter Haynes.

GEORGE L. CARTER RESIDENCE. George Lafayette Carter, known as the "empire builder of Southwest Virginia," was born on January 10, 1857, in Hillsville, Virginia. Self-made, he worked his way up through a number of ventures, becoming a coal and rail magnate and founder of modern Kingsport. He shaped the economic transformation of northeast Tennessee and southwest Virginia. Between 1906 and 1915, Carter lived in Johnson City in this home at Tennessee Avenue and the Locust extension—with the home later becoming part of the ETSU campus.

RESIDENCE OF J. FRED JOHNSON. John Fredrick "J. Fred" Johnson was the head of the Kingsport Improvement Company, Clinchfield land agent, and brother-in-law of George L. Carter. He married Carter's sister, Ruth, on November 18, 1896, in Hillsville, Virginia, the hometown for both. They moved to Johnson City about 1906 and relocated to Kingsport about 1917 when he left his position with Clinchfield to further develop Kingsport into a model town. Because of this work, he was affectionately known and revered as the "father of Kingsport." Johnson lived at 302 Spring Street (on the corner of Spring and Ash) when he first came to Johnson City and then moved to 823 West Locust, near the Carter home. It is likely that the home in this postcard is the one on Locust Street.

J.A. MARTIN RESIDENCE, WATAUGA AVE. James Alexander and Lena Mae Martin lived at 409 East Watauga Avenue from the early 1900s through the 1940s (she passed in 1943, and he in 1947). In 1908, James was in the wholesale lumber business at 227 East Main Street, where Capone's is located today, and later, he was in real estate. His father, J.D. Martin, was a dentist in town in the 1880s.

Eight

HOUSES OF WORSHIP

LITTLE WHITE CHURCH. The First Baptist Church congregation formed on July 3, 1869, with 19 members and Asa Routh and N. Noffsinger serving as the presbytery. They initially met in the Presbyterian church until May 1881 and then moved to the second floor of Science Hill High School. Shortly after this, they purchased a lot for $100 at 224–226 East Main Street, where they erected their first building known as the Little White Church and held the first service on April 7, 1883.

ROAN STREET BAPTIST CHURCH. Roan Street Baptist Church, located at 100 East Watauga Avenue in the former Lusk School building where the Almeda Apartments stand today, split from First Baptist Church over a dispute over the future location of the church. The new church formed on May 8, 1907, with 102 charter members and G.W. Sitton, J.A. Cargille, H.J. Kilby, John H, Bayless, A.P. Whitlock, and R.C. Phillips as deacons; H.A. Reep, clerk; and I.A. Bittle, treasurer. Rev. T.G. Davis accepted the call as pastor in August 1907. The separation ended on April 21, 1910, when both churches adopted an agreement developed jointly by committees from each.

CENTRAL BAPTIST CHURCH. Central Baptist was formed with the reunion of the members of First and Roan Street Baptist Churches in 1910. The church voted to stay in the Roan Street location until a new building was ready and elected Rev. Tom Davis as pastor. A lot was purchased from Isaac Harr and the church moved into its new building in the spring of 1913. Disaster struck on December 27, 1930, when fire damaged the building, resulting in the loss of the dome.

MUNSEY MEMORIAL METHODIST CHURCH. The church began in 1871 as the Market Street Methodist Church. A structure of handmade bricks (located near the site of the current parking lot in front of the Counseling Center) served the congregation until 1908, when the building in the postcard was dedicated. At that time, members chose to rename the church in honor of Rev. William E. Munsey, a brilliant pulpit preacher who died in Jonesboro in 1877 at the age of 44. The church has had a long history of caring for its members (both body and soul) through its services and facilities. Initiatives included creation of the Munsey Club in 1909, providing gym equipment and showers, and in 1949 adding an education building with a swimming pool. In 1955, the beloved round church was demolished for construction of a new sanctuary.

CHRISTIAN CHURCH. The building, located at 335–339 East Main Street, has been modified but retains much of the structure seen in this postcard. The second home for the First Christian Church was dedicated on June 10, 1906, after the first building located at 212–214 East Main Street burned to the ground on May 2, 1905. The church added a Sunday school annex in 1923 and a sanctuary in 1951. In 1972, the First Christian Church moved to a new location, and the Downtown Christian Church took over this location.

ST. JOHN'S EPISCOPAL CHURCH. The "Rock Church," located at 500 North Roan Street, was designed to mimic medieval English architecture and utilized nearby river rock and limestone. The cornerstone for the original church was laid on September 7, 1905. However, the first corporate Episcopal service in Johnson City was held on June 16, 1889. Rev. Samuel Ringgold, rector of St. John's, Knoxville, officiated at the service with 16 people in attendance. Services were held originally in schools and stores until the Lusk School became available.

FIRST PRESBYTERIAN CHURCH. The First
Presbyterian Church was organized in 1882 by
the Reverend Gilbert Gordon with 24 charter
members. Like all the other early churches, it first
met in the homes of members such as Mr. and Mrs.
W.W. Faw and then the schoolhouse and the First
Methodist Church. A lot at 234 North Roan Street
was purchased, and the building was dedicated in
March 1890. In 1947, a new location was selected
farther north on Roan, where the current building
is located.

WATAUGA AVENUE PRESBYTERIAN CHURCH. On September 27, 1892, a small group wanting
to affiliate with the "Northern" United Presbyterian Church in the United States of America
(UPCUSA) denomination organized the Second Presbyterian Church. For the first two years,
services were held at local schools. The church name was changed to Watauga Avenue on May
14, 1894, when the charter was signed. In 1896, a small brick chapel was built and dedicated at
the corner of Watauga Avenue and New Street. In 1966, it became one of the early integrated
churches in the city when 26 members of Bethesda Presbyterian (founded in 1899) joined the
church when theirs closed.

FIRST METHODIST CHURCH. The First Methodist Episcopal Church was organized in 1865 and held services at the Brush Creek schoolhouse, later the homesite of Isaac Harr. In 1868, members moved their services to Science Hill and, on May 19, 1883, into their first owned sanctuary at 232 East Main Street. They stayed in this location until 1907, when they built a yellow brick sanctuary (left) at the corner of Main and Roan Streets (the present-day location of the King's Centre Building). This structure served them until 1927, when they sold the property to Sam Sells, who built the King's Department Store at the location. After worshipping for two years at the junior high school, the congregation moved into its new redbrick structure (below), located at 900 Spring Street on May 12, 1929, where the congregation worships to this day.

Tacoma Church of God

Parkway at Wendover Drive, Johnson City, Tenn.
Rev. Dan Harman, Pastor

TACOMA CHURCH OF GOD. This large church facility is located at 1005 John Exum Parkway near the intersection with Wendover Drive. The church dates to 1917, when the congregation purchased land on the corner of Maple and Roan Streets for its first building. However, in 1927, the city wanted to relocate Columbus Powell School to that location and traded the church property located on Tacoma Avenue. The current site for the church was purchased in 1957.

"OUR CHURCH." The First Church of the Brethren sanctuary, located at the corner of East Chilhowie Avenue and Elm Street at 301 Chilhowie, was dedicated on January 28, 1928. It stood at this location until 1970, when the building was demolished for the construction of what is now Interstate 26 (it was State Route 137 and then designated Interstate 181 from 1985 to 2007). In this location, the entire 300 block of Chilhowie Avenue was lost to the interstate.

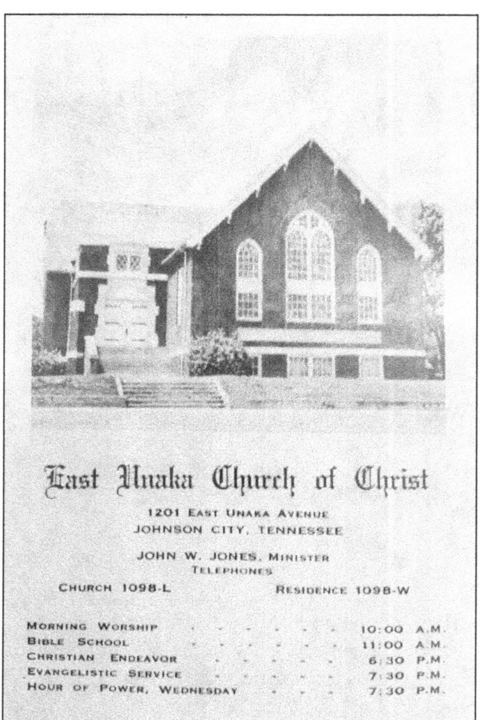

Mission House. One of the first Roman Catholic priests to minister in East Tennessee, Fr. Emmanuel Francis Callahan was ordained on June 29, 1897. He spent many years serving the missions of East Tennessee and would visit the Mission House to hold Mass and Catechism the first Sunday of every month. The Missions of St. Francis de Sales covered a seven-county area and had a mission house behind Science Hill High School on East Market Street.

Nine

PASTIMES

JOHN ROBINSON SHOW. Traveling circuses regularly rolled into Johnson City from the late 19th century well into the 20th century. The John Robinson Circus toured from 1842 until 1911 and was one of the longest-running family-owned circuses in the United States. This postcard features one of the main attractions for a circus at the turn of the century, elephants. The crowds, unaccustomed to such large, exotic animals, watched them with exhilaration and fear alike—depending upon the unruliness of the elephants. This photograph shows the parade of pachyderms in front of the Bee Hive, located at 207–209 East Main Street, as the procession heads west where it would eventually make its way over to Walnut Street.

JULY 4, 1908 AND 1910. Fourth of July parades were always popular and welcome events each summer for a number of years. The photograph below from 1910 shows the Model Mill Company wagon at the front of the parade column. It is carrying sacks of flour lined in a row. The local newspaper, the *Comet*, reported this big parade started promptly at 10:00 a.m., the weather was ideal, and "nobody got shot and very few half-shot and there were no casualties." The parade was "led by the fife and drum corps from the Soldiers' Home and immediately behind it came the Confederate veterans under the command of Capt. W.A. Dickenson and dressed as they were when they returned, from the war. This is the first time, in all probability, that the grey veterans ever marched to music to a blue-coated band; heretofore they have either run from or to it."

BARNUM & BAILEY CIRCUS. The Greatest Show on Earth visited Johnson City on October 8, 1909. This photograph was taken across the street from J.G. Sterchi Furniture Company at 225 East Main Street, where it sold furniture, stoves, carpets, rugs, and a complete line of undertaker's goods. The September 30, 1909, edition of the *Comet* contains a large ad for the show advertising 1,280 persons, 700 horses, 40 elephants, a family of giraffes, the only two-horned rhinos in captivity, and 100 acts, including Karolly's Great German Horse Circus, 60 aerialists and acrobats, and 50 clowns all arriving in 85 double-length railcars. The spectacle was so large, it was held in six arenas and the Hippodrome.

LADY OF THE FOUNTAIN. The Lady of the Fountain statue, an icon in downtown during the first part of the 20th century, was placed in the public square, which came to be known as Fountain Square from that point on. It was removed about 1937 to accommodate parking and traffic improvements around the square. At that point, the statue minus the fountain base was placed at Memorial Stadium for half a dozen years and then ended up out of state until the city repurchased it and returned it home in 1983. A bronze replica of the original statue was placed at Fountain Square in April 2011 to once again be enjoyed by Johnson Citians.

UNAKA SPRINGS HOTEL. Folks from Johnson City could take a short trip to relax in the outdoors while staying at this affordable mountain lodge next to the Nolichuckey River in Unicoi County. The CC&O had a stop at Unaka Springs that was about an hour and fifteen minutes' journey. Room-rental rates for the first couple of decades of the 20th century ranged from $2 a day to $30 a month, and the proprietor, A.V. Deaderick, a well-known photographer, also operated a studio there.

A SCENE AT HUNTER'S CAMP ON THE WATAUGA RIVER. The Watauga River rises from a spring near the base of Peak Mountain at Linville Gap in Avery County, North Carolina, and runs almost 79 miles to its end at its confluence with the Holston River's South Fork. The Watauga is considered one of the best trout-fishing destinations in the Southern Appalachians. As for hunting, the area was known for plentiful grouse, quail, dove, duck, rabbits, and squirrels.

ELKS HOME. The Elks home was located on the third floor of the Armbrust-Smith Building (corner of Spring and Tipton Streets) prior to relocating to the club's own building at 113 Spring Street. The Benevolent and Protective Order of Elks (BPOE) was founded in 1868 in New York City, and later developed into a fraternal service organization. Johnson City was home to several fraternal organizations at the time this postcard was published, including the Eagles, Masons, and Knights of Pythias.

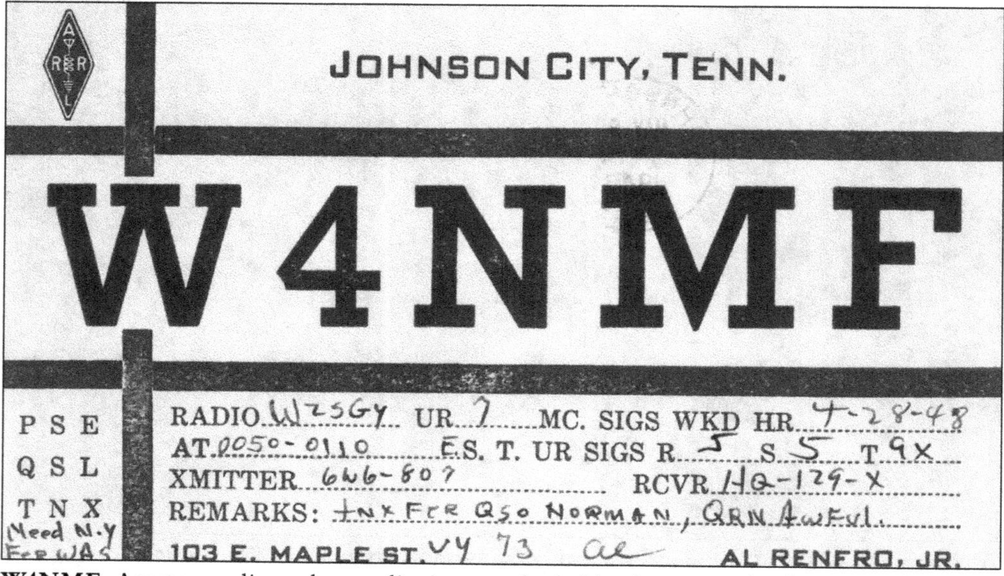

W4NMF. Amateur radio, or ham radio, is a popular hobby that uses radio frequency spectrums for the non-commercial exchange of communication. This QSL card was mailed by Al Renfro Jr. to Norman Katz in New York City to confirm two-way radio contact between their stations. Collecting these cards became popular with radio operators in the 1920s and 1930s.

COUNTRY CLUB AND CLUBHOUSE. The Johnson City Country Club was incorporated on September 3, 1913, by five charter members: George T. Wofford, Allen Harris, Lee. F. Miller, H.L. White, and A.B. Crouch. In 1914, a temporary nine-hole course and small cabin were built on 60 acres leased from Harry D. Gump. After raising funds through the Watauga Corporation, the members purchased six tracts of land on January 1 and June 15, 1920, followed by construction of the first nine holes and the clubhouse. After adding a golf pro shop, the club was in full operation by the end of 1921.

ROOSEVELT STADIUM. Football has been a favorite pastime since 1914, when Johnson City High School fielded its first team. The need for better facilities was met when Roosevelt Stadium (later renamed Memorial Stadium) opened in 1935. It was originally named for Pres. Franklin Roosevelt because the facility was partially funded by Works Progress Administration (WPA) money, as well as by funding from several people who offered the city $1,000 loans for the project. The stadium was located at 540 East Main Street but was demolished in July 2010 to make way for a new community center.

GRADUATION DANCE INVITATION. Postcards have long been used as a quick means of communication. This card was sent by Margaret Ann Howard to Jimmy Joe Hartsell inviting him to an informal dance at the American Legion Hut, Tuesday, May 28, 1946. The American Legion Hut was located at 503 East Main Street.

JIM MOONEY. James I. "Jim" Mooney, a three-sport star for East Tennessee State Teacher's College in the mid-1920s, was best known for his feats on a baseball diamond. After starting for East Tennessee State, he played for the New York Giants and St. Louis Cardinals, pitching in the fourth game of the 1934 World Series with the Cardinals. Mooney returned to East Tennessee State as a baseball coach in 1939, retiring in 1966 after 23 seasons. He was inducted into the school's hall of fame in 1977, and the old baseball field was named for him, but it was razed for construction of the new soccer stadium, which opened in 2008.

THE WILLIAMS SISTERS. Carrie and Betty Williams started singing gospel at a young age and performed in area churches. Carrie played guitar and sang alto, and Betty sang soprano. This card, originally published by the Asheville Post Card Company (1910–1977), was used to advertise the duo.

BUFFALO MOUNTAIN METHODIST CAMP. This nearly 500-acre summer camp, located at 201 Methodist Camp Road in Jonesborough, was opened in 1947 and operated by the Holston Conference of the United Methodist Church until 2012. In August 2012, the camp and surrounding community were devastated by a flash flood that led to the camp being relocated and the property sold as conservation land. For many years, the fifth graders at University School would spend a week at the camp hiking, rappelling, and playing games at the camp.

THE WILLMARY SHOP. This gift and antique store, located at 102 Willmary Road at the intersection of US Route 11E just north of the William DeVault Bridge over Boone Lake in Piney Flats, was opened in 1954 by William Weldon and Mary Ava (née Snyder) DeVault and was open in this location for many years.

Ten

GREETINGS FROM JOHNSON CITY

GREETINGS FROM JOHNSON CITY.
With Johnson City flourishing as
a center of industry and commerce
and having two colleges and the
Soldiers' Home, the need to send a
quick note home had never been in
greater demand. This card features
five miniature scenes from the area,
including an early view of the high
school. This PCK Series postcard
was published by Paul C. Koeber Co.
(1900–1923) for J.E. Crouch. John
Edwin Crouch was superintendent
of city schools in 1908 and owned a
bookstore at 219 and then 217 East
Main Street, where later the Darling
Shop and Hart's Jeweler/Betty Gay
were located respectively. Both
buildings are now being renovated.

GREETINGS FROM A BUTTERFLY SIREN. Another of Crouch's publications, this card features two miniature scenes from the Soldiers' Home, a view of Watauga Avenue, and an early view of the Christian church nestled in butterfly wings protruding from the back of a robed woman. Crouch's advertised "a line of high grade post cards," as well as books, school supplies, Kodak albums, and Waterman's Ideal Fountain Pens.

"JOHNSON CITY, TENN." Another in the series published by J.E. Crouch, this card features a mini postcard of Main Street on an easel mounted to a chalkboard with a young student having just finished writing a message. The message extols the virtues of Johnson City including "genuine Tennessee hospitality and lots of pretty girls. Be sure to meet them at Crouch's Book Store." (Frank Tannewitz Jr. collection.)

118

"EVERYBODY IS DOING IT IN JOHNSON CITY, TENN." The first souvenir postcard printed in the United States was created in 1893 to advertise the World's Columbian Exposition in Chicago. Initially, the post office was the only establishment allowed to print postcards, and it held a monopoly until May 19, 1898, when Congress passed the Private Mailing Card Act, which allowed private publishers and printers to produce postcards.

"THE GIRLS CAN KEEP THINGS TO THEMSELVES IN JOHNSON CITY." During the "undivided back" era of postcards, cards were not allowed to have a divided back, and only the front could be written upon. On March 1, 1907, the post office allowed correspondents to write on the reverse of a postcard, which was now allowed to have a divided back to follow suit with the very popular style of European postcards. This change ushered in the birth of the "modern postcard" or "golden age" of postcards, making them the equivalent of social networking on the web today.

"HOLDING DOWN THE LAW" AND "I'M HAVING A 'H' OF A TIME" IN JOHNSON CITY. The following eight postcards were published by the Rotograph Company (1904–1911) as part of a large series of comic and somewhat risqué images and slogans that could be custom ordered by a retailer for its city. Postcards of this type could be purchased in bulk from 30¢ for 50 cards to $5 for 1,000 cards. It is unknown how many different images were available in this Rotograph series, but the author has at least 33 different Johnson City images.

120

"THE BUSINESS CENTRE" AND "HOT STUFF" FROM JOHNSON CITY. There is no indication of who ordered or distributed these postcards on the reverse of any of the cards in this collection. However, with images of lax police, bottles of alcohol, and fetching women, perhaps Al Capone was a recipient of a few of these postcards, spurring his later interest in the city.

"A Tasty Article" and "It's Hard to Get Away" from Johnson City.
Located at 684 Broadway in New York City, Rotograph was one of the major publishers at the turn of the 20th century. The company was founded by Germans who took over the National Art Views Company in 1904 to obtain access to previously published American images that were ready for quick republication.

122

"RAISED" AND "A KISS FROM EVERYBODY" IN JOHNSON CITY. The "Kiss" postcard image is reminiscent of the Gibson Girl, who was the "personification of the feminine ideal of beauty" as portrayed by the pen-and-ink illustrations of Charles Dana Gibson in the late 19th and early 20th centuries. The artist saw his creation as representing the composite of "thousands of American girls." The first celebrity Gibson Girl was Irene Langhorne, a prominent suffragette and sister of Lady Nancy Astor. Langhorne later married Charles Gibson and cofounded Big Sisters, Inc., which helped girls in trouble.

LARGE-LETTER GREETINGS. Both of these large-letter linen postcards feature scenes from Johnson City or other parts of Tennessee within each large-sized letter. The heyday of large-letter postcards was the 1930s through the 1950s, which parallels the "linen era" of postcards. The card above was printed by Curt Teich for Zimmerman & Torbett News Agency, and the one below was printed by the Asheville Post Card Co., a prolific publisher in the South.

COUNTRY AND CITY GREETINGS. Both of these postcards were printed by Dexter Press out of West Nyack, New York, but the street scene was published by Haynes Distributing Co. in Roanoke, Virginia. The card above includes a cheesecake photograph of a redheaded "fisherman's dream" as well as other mountain stream fishing images. A promotional pamphlet titled *The Land of the Long Rifles* advertises fishing in any number of lakes, rivers, and mountain streams, teaming with small and largemouth bass, brook (speckled), and rainbow and brown trout just a short drive from modern accommodations. The card below is another view of the most photographed intersection and street corner in Johnson City postcard history and appears to date to the 1950s.

THE SIMPLE LIFE. Published by Taylor, Platt & Company (1906–1916), this postcard plays up Johnson City as an idyllic place. This is something the chamber of commerce and its forerunner, the Commercial Club, have done for many years, with slogans such as "Gateway to the Appalachians," "Queen City of the Mountains," "Where History and Scenery Meet," "The Land of the Long Rifles," and "The American Ruhr," among many others.

WOODEN POSTCARD. Wooden postcards have been available in the United States as keepsakes since at least 1904, when they were sold at the St. Louis World's Fair in Forest Park. Many early wooden postcards were printed with colored images, while others were marked by pyrography or a combination of the two processes. This postcard, featuring a patriotic etching of a saluting soldier, has a "3 Cent Stamp" box on the back, which dates the production of this card to between 1932 and 1958, when one-ounce postage was 3¢.

Bibliography

Bailey, Jr., William P. *History of First United Methodist Church of Johnson City, Tennessee 1865–1990*. Johnson City, TN: Overmountain Press, 1990.

Burleson, David Sinclair. *History of East Tennessee State College*. 1947

Calloway, Brenda C. *America's First Western Frontier, East Tennessee: A Story of the Early Settlers and Indians of East Tennessee*. Johnson City, TN: Overmountain Press, 1989.

Canaday, James. *History of Central Baptist Church, Johnson City, Tennessee: In Celebration of the 100th Anniversary 1869-1969*. Bristol, TN: Preston Printing, 1969.

Cornwell, Cynthia A. *Beside the Waters of the Buffalo: A History of Milligan College to 1941*. Milligan College, TN: Milligan College History Project, 1989.

Cox, Joyce, and W. Eugene Cox. *History of Washington County, Tennessee*. Johnson City, TN: Overmountain Press, 2001.

Ferro, Tony. *Johnson City Country Club: A Centennial Celebration*. Johnson City, TN: Shell Media, 2012.

Groce, W. Todd. *Mountain Rebels: East Tennessee Confederates and the Civil War, 1860–1870*. Knoxville: University of Tennessee Press, 1999.

Hill's Johnson City (Washington County, Tenn.) Directory. Richmond, VA: Hill Directory Company, 1935.

Johnson City, Tennessee City Directory. Asheville, NC: Piedmont Directory/Commercial Service Company, 1908–1909, 1909–1910, 1913, 1917, 1919, 1921, 1925, 1928, 1930, 1932–1933.

Loveday, Jan E. *Milligan College*. Charleston, SC: Arcadia Publishing, 2011.

Stahl, Ray. *A Beacon to Health Care, The Story of the Johnson City Medical Center Hospital*. Kingsport, TN: Printing Concepts, Inc., 1989.

———. *Greater Johnson City: A Pictorial History*. Virginia Beach, VA: The Donning Company/Publishers, 1983.

Williams, Frank B. *East Tennessee State University: A University's Story, 1911–1980*. Johnson City: East Tennessee State University Press, 1940.

Williams, Samuel Cole. *History of Johnson City and its Environs*. Johnson City, TN: The Watauga Press, 1940.

Williams, Virginia. *History of First Presbyterian Church, Johnson City, Tennessee*. Johnson City, TN: Young's Printing and Bindery, 1994.

Discover Thousands of Local History Books Featuring Millions of Vintage Images

Arcadia Publishing, the leading local history publisher in the United States, is committed to making history accessible and meaningful through publishing books that celebrate and preserve the heritage of America's people and places.

Find more books like this at
www.arcadiapublishing.com

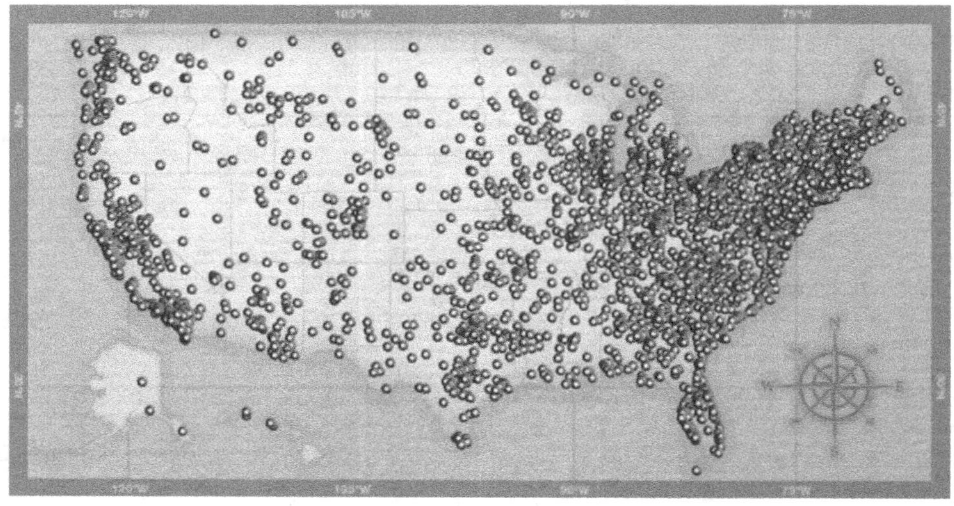

Search for your hometown history, your old stomping grounds, and even your favorite sports team.